Surveillance
Basic's for Ten Bucks

Details on how one might begin, conduct, photograph, and report on a surveillance investigation on foot or moving.

The Investigator who will be telling you about surveillance is Charles E. Neuf who has 40 years' experience of working investigations at every level of Police and the Private Sector.

25 years of this time, he was a working as a licensed Private Detective in three States.

The Investigator was a Surveillance specialist and at one time having 22 vehicles, cars; trucks, cycles, and a boat he used in his uncover surveillance operations.

The Investigators Promise, I will be telling you;
What worked for me for 25 years.
1. About Investigators & Surveillances
2. Skills that might help you.
3. Basic Tools you will need.
4. Who might want Surveillances & Why.
5. Give you ideas on How to start the Surveillance
6. Tips on walking, moving & vehicle Surveillance.
7. Some ideas on Photographing & Surveillance.

In other words, just about everything The Investigator has learned over the late 40 years and used about How to start your Surveillance, tools you will need, tricks to use in different kinds of surveillances and how to stay out of trouble.

This series is offered as an alternative to trial and error. The Investigator would hope it would speed a newcomer in setting up, running and reporting on the surveillance and help, them avoid serious pitfalls.

Written in an easy to read format, more like you are sitting at a coffee shop taking to a friend. Much of the "How To" will be told in short stories just like it happened for The Investigator.

Every effort has been made to avoid theory and stick to proven methods and procedures that will provide a firm foundation on which one can build their surveillance techniques on. The material presented is slanted toward the practical knowledge.

Copyright

No part of this book may be reproduced in any form without permission in writing

Copyright Charles E, Neuf, Bradenton, Florida

Author Charles E. Neuf CPP,

ISBN 978-1-79472-544-7 90000

This book is designed to provide information about the subject matter covered. The "Short Stories included" are written to the best of the Writers recall on a subject taking place many years ago, but personally experienced by the Writer at the time the event took place.

The Voices telling some of the stories are from the past. The writer calls his writings "Creative Non- Fiction Writing Based on The Investigators Real Cases."

The purpose of this book is to educate and entertain, there may be mistakes both typographical and in content. The author / publisher has neither liability nor responsibility to any person or entity with respect to any loss or damage caused or alleged to be caused directly or indirectly by information contained in this book.

Since the stories in this book are real experiences involving the writer/storyteller and the purpose of the writer, is documentation and entertainment of the reader, Conversations "quoted" are what the storyteller imaged they were at the time.

Contents

The Investigator,
Background, & Writing Style,

Before becoming a State Trooper in 1959, the Time Traveler/Writer was a Farmer, Forest Fire Fighter, and Railroad laborer, Coalminer, Trucker, and a Merchant Marine on Inland waterway Towboats as a licensed Tankerman, among many other things.

As an Illinois State Trooper, the Writer Started Patrol duty in the Chicago, Illinois area, a population of eleven million. In the next 16 years, he would be a State Police Detective, LEIU Agent, State Police Training Instructor, and Confidante to three Illinois Governors.

After Leaving the State Police, Trooper Neuf became a licensed Private Detective in three States. He became a Certified Protection Profession (CPP), working Private Investigations Nationwide for Attorneys, Corporations, and Governmental.

The Time Traveler, Investigator/Writer/Storyteller, began writing short stories in the 1960's. He has published over sixty books and e-Books of short stories based on his life and observations of life.

The purpose of all writings is to share the Time Travelers personal experiences and knowledge. What he acquired in his travels through time and space, with others who may have like interests and beliefs.

Over a period of forty years, the writer had written hundreds of investigation reports. First as a State Police Detective and then a Private Detective. Each report had to tell an easy to understand a story about something he had been involved in.

After entering the private sector, he wrote his first book, an instruction manual on "How To Get Information," using the freedom of information act.

This was later expanded into a seminar for Police, Private Investigators, Attorneys, and Banks; finally, it ended up in a college as part of a Criminal Justice Course.

"Sometimes letting things go is an act of far greater power than defending or hanging on."

— Eckhart Tolle, A New Earth: Awakening to Your Life's Purpose

Preface

877 Words, Est. Reading Times 5 to 10 minutes

Let us, you the reader and me, the Investigator and your mentor, get things straight between us before we start. I am your friend, your guide, a person who will be with you when you start your first Surveillance.

Yes, you could go to college and take a criminal Justice Course, but there are drawbacks to doing that.

1. It will take you two years to finish the course.

2. In all likelihood the Instructor, at best maybe an Ex Policeman, they may have even instructed Police.

3. We are not talking about being police officer; we are talking about working the other side of the fence. We will most likely be bordering on the edge of the law ourselves when we do things.

4. Police arrest people, put them behind bars. The P.I. maybe working to get them out from behind bars, Police and P.I.'s are two different species.

5. The P.I. in most cases does not care and should not care if their client goes to jail. The P.I's job is usually to do a job the Police will not do, are do not want to do.

6. Well, that is the facts, a P.I. is shady in the eyes of Police, and they are a knight in shining armor to their client. The P.I. is paid for what they do, Police are paid no matter what they do, and if things go bad, they are put on Paid Leave. If things go bad for a P.I., they are out of business and may even be in Jail.

Well Back to what we were talking about.

The "Ten Bucks" series of writings are prepared for the person who desires to enter the field of investigation. They will be of equal interest and value to one who has already entered the investigation profession and may be having problems generating sufficient clientele and providing enough services to become financially stable.

Above all, it will assist the novices who in increasing numbers today want to enter the private investigation field. These newcomers look about for a guide, a textbook, a manual, or some sort of help to assist them in entering the field of private investigation; and they find little available.

For whatever reason, private investigation has not received the attention it merits either in law enforcement literature, seminars, or correspondence courses.

As a result, each beginner is left alone to find his own way, conduct his own training, devise his own system, work his own solutions, and in the process needlessly repeats many dangerous mistakes already experienced by professional investigators.

This series is offered as a substitute for trial and error. I would hope it would speed a newcomer to a professional status and help him avoid serious pitfalls that have cost too many a career in the private sector investigation.

Every effort has been made to avoid theory and stick to proven methods and procedures that will provide a firm foundation on which one can build a satisfying career as a professional investigator.

The material presented is slanted toward the practical knowledge, which the Private Investigator needs to begin and base his career upon. Guidelines for action will be offered but I emphasis will be placed upon the individual skills of each investigator, his sixth sense, steady judgment, and ability to make the correct decisions.

The book Enter: The World of the Private Investigator is a large book cover most of the skills of a P.I.. This book targets how one may enter the profession of the private investigator, conduct his business, obtain clients, give guidelines to reasonable prices, and provide basic knowledge for the new investigator to begin his career. Enter the World of Private Detective can be purchased at lulu books under the name of Charles Neuf CPP.

It is the individual responsibility of one who enters the investigation field to acquire skills to communicate with people and graciously solve problems.

Throughout the Ten Buck series, there will be references toward legal opinions, interpretations, judicial rulings, court proceedings, statutes, operational standards and other references presented solely for their value as illustrations. Reference to this material is no implication, and there may be no inference that they are universally applicable.

"What a liberation to realize that the "voice in my head" is not who I am. Who am I then? The one who sees that."

― Eckhart Tolle, *A New Earth: Awakening to Your Life's Purpose*

"Don't let a mad world tell you that success is anything other than a successful present moment."

How the Material will be Presented, "Talking with the Investigator"

The writing style of the author; is that of a friend and mentor. The writer is The Investigator, so when the writer talks to you most of the time he will be using, I, or me that is because it is me, The Investigator that is talking to you.

Envision yourself seated at a table with a cup of coffee or a soda. You and the Investigator are talking about an incident that occurred while you were on an investigation.

Detectives, Investigators, and all people who have to use their imagination in their profession have times when they have to put themselves into the character they want answers from.

You are the reader, now sit down, relate just as you are really sitting at an outdoor coffee shop having a conversation with The Investigator. He talks to you, you listen as if he is there, then you talk back. That is how this book is written, The Investigator is talking to you, you listen, and then you talk back about what we are talking about.

You and I are having a discussion about "how to" handle this occurrence and your friend the Investigator, is relating to you his experiences, from his 40 years of handling Police and Security matters.

The Investigator wants to help you solve some of the perplexing problems a P.I. faces. He is being honest with you, by relating things he knows can happen. The Investigator knows that not all problems have the same set of circumstances; therefore, circumstances sometimes change the action to take.

He knows no one can give you an action, to take for

everything that happens, therefore; the action you take is based on your decision. What the Investigator wants to do is share his experiences and knowledge with you, so you will have something to base your actions on.

The Writing Plan;

The Mission; each chapter will start with a mission of what we want to accomplish, in the chapter.

Then, what we will talk about; what we will talk about in the chapter.

A Scenario; a scenario is a story; a story or reference about the subject that you can relate to.

Details; this will be about the subject and some things you can do.

This writing plan, will give you an understanding, of what we will be covering in each chapter; it also keeps The Investigator on track when he is writing.

"I love it when a plan comes to-gather"; do you know what TV Series that quote came from? (The "A Team")

What would you have done differently?

Questions you might ask yourself about the last Scenario story about The Investigators case, What would you have done based on your past Experiences and Knowledge?

Now, you are the Investigator, Start with writing down anything you are ask, "Any Question" about as anything by the Investigator, got a recorder after writing, dictate any thoughts you have to your little hand held recorder. Then later listen to it, Does It Make Sense?

Promise 1 Chapter One

About Investigators & Surveillance

The Mission; *each chapter will start with a mission of what we want to accomplish, in the chapter.*

In this chapter we will be talking about people who conduct surveillances and why.

Then some things about surveillances a person should know about before they start a surveillance.

A Scenario; *a scenario is a story; a story or reference about the subject that you can relate to.*

The surveillance investigation your thinking about toiday involves a suspected wayward husband who may be spending time with an unknown person.

Details; this will be about the subject and some things you can do.

This surveillance starts with only the details about who is suspected of doing something and you need information before you can start.

This writing plan, *will give you an understanding, of what we will be covering in each chapter; it also keeps The Investigator on track when he is writing.*

"I love it when a plan comes to-gather"; do you know what TV Series that quote came from? (The "A Team")

What would you have done differently?

At the end of the chapter you might ask yourself, what would you have done based on your past Experiences and Knowledge?

Now, you are the Investigator, Start with writing

down anything you are ask, "Any Question" about as anything about the Investigation, got a recorder after writing, dictate any thoughts you have to your little hand held recorder. Then later listen to it, before you start, Does It Make Sense?

Investigators & Surveillance

567 Words, Reading Times 3 to 6 Minutes

There seems to be some confusion on the part of those who use investigation services in choosing an investigator.

Much depends on the mindset of the individual searching for the investigator. This is a subject that is of vital interest to the end user of investigation services and I felt that we should briefly discuss your choice of an investigator or before starting an investigation yourself.

The user's mind set varies from deep emotion to a clear cut business approach of price. But whatever your mind set when you obtained an investigator, keep in mind the ultimate goal and desired results you would like to have.

**The Key is What Do You Want To Happen, in other words why are you doing this?*

Investigators and investigation agencies are specialists, and to be considered a specialist and an expert, one must be trained and have experience.

There is very little actual training that can be obtained concerning surveillances, observations, and activity reports. It all boils down to first hand knowlege of, "How To."

The biggest factor to be considered is the experience of the individual investigator who is heading up the operation and the quality of the investigator who is conducting the field investigation.

Because of the considerations for quality in investigation, price can only be a secondary consideration to the user. It is the experience and equipment of the investigation organization that will produce results.

So when choosing your investigator or investigation agency, weigh the importance of your surveillance, observation or activity report in a dollar and cents fashion.

If it is really not rewarding enough to conduct a proper surveillance and pay the fee that is required for the experienced investigator, perhaps you should not obtain investigation services at all.

When you make your first contact with the investigation agency, inquire as to the amount of time this agency has been in business in the given area where you need the services and into the quality of the investigator who will be responsible for the investigation itself.

Do not be tricked by low prices and receive a security guard or minimum wage person as your field investigator. Inquire about the type of equipment that will be used.

Does the organization have specially equipped surveillance vehicles?

Do the investigators in the field have years of experience in this type of investigation?

Is the camera equipment of professional quality?

Most of all, who is responsible, for the overall layout, of the investigation?

Once you have decided this is the investigator for you, and your purposes, rely on that investigator, as you would your Attorney, your Accountant, or a Health Specialist who has your best interest at heart.

Surveillance Investigations

Surveillance investigations are the most used services of Private Detectives in the private sector. Much information can be obtained from observation and surveillance of individuals or locations.

Yet, surveillance investigations require more specialized equipment, manpower, and experience than any other area of investigation.

This specialized area of investigation is the most difficult, demanding, time consuming and expensive of all investigation techniques.

Considering all the needs for surveillance investigation, there is one element we have not touched upon, and that is the productivity of such an investigation.

Surveillance is the most expensive, non,—productive investigation technique that can be used. And yet in many instances it is the only investigation technique available.

In most instances, a client requesting a surveillance investigation has only one opportunity to obtain the information.

If the investigator is not highly experienced and well equipped, the probability of gaining this information is seriously affected.

Well that's it about Surveillances and Investigators what you have just talked to the Investigator about how he looks at surveillance and the investigator, you might have different ideas, if some write them down.

Now The Investigator would like to tell you a story about two surveillances he once ran.

Surveillance The Wandering Husband

"Hi, I'm Charlie in Springfield and I was checking our phone log and see that you called our office twice to speak to me, and I didn't get an answer when I recalled.

"Who did you say you are?"

"Charlie Neuf, Chief Investigator, with the Investigators Detective Agency in Springfield."

"Yes, I called some time ago, and told the person I spoke to I didn't want to talk on the telephone about private matters."

"Where do you live, what city?"

"I live a 100 miles south of you near Effingham."

"If you would want me to come and see you I have an hourly fee of $45.00 an hour and 40 cents a mile for travel. I estimate that would cost you $250.00."

"That will be fine, I have tomorrow morning free, and would 10am be good for you?"

"10am would be fine, I'll need directions."

10am was not fine, but I needed the work, so if it means getting up at 6am, I'll do it.

From the sound of our conversation this lady was used to being in charge, I'd guess a female professional, a Doctor, Lawyer, or Business owner and there is something in her life she cannot control.

I got up at six, got ready to go, and stopped at the Sunrise for breakfast and it was eight before I left town.

I wasn't use to this early morning traffic, so it looks like I'll be running late for my appointment.

"Your 20 minutes late." Was the greeting from this well dressed lady in her late 50's, but she invited me in anyway.

"According to my speedometer, it was 120 miles, it took a few minutes longer than planned," I replied.

"Let's get right down to it; I have a wandering husband and I need to know where he is going."

"Do you have an idea of when this happens, any details of any kind?"

"I have details, location, and an idea it will be a nurse from the hospital."

"It will be on a Tuesday or Thursday, from eight in the morning to two in the afternoon.

"And how do you know this?" I thought she would say because I followed him or I had someone else follow him.

"I check his speedometer on his car after he goes to the hospital a round trip is exactly 15 miles, but on Tuesday and

Thursday he drives 18 miles."

"Alright, so you want to know where he is going on Tuesday and Thursday is that right?"

"Yes, and I want pictures."

"I think I'll have ten hours a day involved and a total of 450 miles, just estimating it will cost about $500 a day, I'll need a retainer of a $1000."

Again, I a-s-s-u-m-e-d she would say too much, I would collect my $250 for the trip and be on my way.

"Will you take one check for to-day and the two days investigation?"

"Yes and when would you like me to start?"

"Tomorrow, I'll give you the details about him and a special phone number to call me at between six and eight PM."

Well this is something I needed, but didn't want, today while I was gone, Linda ran a background on the lady I met with this morning.

Very Interesting; The new client and her husband are a Medical practice in their community and have been for the last ten years. They have their own Medical Building as well as a home in town and a farm nearby.

Now this is serious, my client describes her husband and business partner as a wandering husband. What does that mean?

There is no emotion involved in the statement or how she said it, it sounds like a business statement, she understands what is going on and how it will affect the finances or he is just wandering?

Well my new client was all business and knew what she wanted, where he should be going, and she wanted pictures as documentation.

There was no mention of a name of whom he was meeting. She knows who he is meeting is a nurse, and she does not care, it did not matter, why not, wives always wants to know who the other person of interest is, strange! This bothers me, but I don't know why?

I found a little Mom & Pop Motel left over from the 1950's just outside of town and took a room for two nights.

At heart I am an old fashion guy, I like little businesses, local restaurants, and little motels, all with some history.

You don't see too many of these old post World War Two, "over niters" any more. It was designed for traveling families that took to the road in their new 1946 Chevrolet Wagon;

It was before the Eisenhower Freeways were built after the war, and everything was two lane roads from the late 1930's and speeds traveled were 45 or 50 miles per hour. This was before the interstate and speeds of 70 MPH went into effect.

Each little cabin in the motel court has a little carport, with a side door that allows you to step out of the cabin and get into your car in the event of foul weather. This place reminds me of one of my first State Police investigations in Springfield that involved a couple of mob bosses from East St. Louis and Chicago meeting half way to settle a territory problem, only that motel had little garages.

Anyway that case cost one of them their legs when a bomb when off in their car as they were leaving.

Inside you have a small eating area, lounge with a sleep bed couch, and bedroom. Everything a family of four traveling would need for an overnight rest.

What I will be doing is following the doctor to find out what he might be doing to put that extra three miles on the car on Tuesday and Thursday.

In my training series, I wrote a training manual for investigators that give a more indepth understanding about the How and Why of surveillance. Surveillance is least productive and most expensive tool of investigation.

I was setting near the doctor's house at 7am, just in the event something changed the time element my client based her information on.

Getting ready for surveillance is half the job. There are supplies you need to be able to stay in the car for long periods of time and the tools you need at hand to do the job.

I had stopped at a Quick Stop gas station the night before and picked up a few items I might need and packed my car for all day surveillance, a gallon of water, and Zip lock bags for the bathroom, black out curtains for the backseat of the car.

In the back seat I had two F-1 Cannon Auto wind Cameras, one loaded with 400 ASA, and the other with 1000 ASA for low light, levels and an overnight bag in the event I might stay over.

At 8am, the garage door opens and a Blue Olds, 4dr backs out into the street and heads south. It's a small town and there aren't too many cars on the streets, this makes following someone a bit more difficult, but we made it to the hospital without arousing any suspicion.

Again, parking on the street near the hospital parking lot is risky, cars in and out, hospital employees walking around, each person looks at you as if they are asking what are you doing, just sitting in the car looking around?

Four hours later the target is out and leaving the parking lot, he heads north on the highway out of town to the Country Club golf course, where a sign in front advertise they are having a three day golf tournament.

Two hours later he is back at the office, I set on him until five and leave and go to my room at the old over niter Motel.

I phone Linda and ask if she will meet me half way with a station wagon, I wouldn't last another day in this small town with the same car on surveillance.

When I down sized I kept a couple extra cars for things like this, I specialize in undetected surveillances, and I'm good at it and have the equipment needed to do it.

Linda and I met at a little restaurant about half way between Springfield and Effingham, had dinner, and switched cars. I needed the Chevy station wagon because it is setup with curtains to blackout the back and I can sit for hours without exposure to anyone moving around the car,

I can see them, but they can't see me and I can photograph out the windows using high speed film.

About investigators and their vehicles, what the investigator drives on an investigation is one of the most important tools he will be using on an investigation.

The next morning the same scenario, out at 8am to the hospital parking, inside until 12:30, and then there was a change.

He made a stop at a liquor store, another stop at a food store, and then heading east out of town to a State Park and stopping at a picnic table by the lake shore.

This was perfect for the surveillance. I parked about a hundred yards away looking over the picnic table and the parking area. With my 80-200mm lens, I could get pictures of the people and area they are in.

15 minutes later, I'm sitting in the back of the station wagon and a small car pulls in and parks, an attractive long haired blond gets out.

Click, click click, she goes over to the picnic table, the man stands up and the two embrace, click, click, click, click, then they kiss, click, click, click, click, I've have the photographs I need as evidence.

I can't believe it. It would normally take four or five days to get the car, the license plate, the girl, the embrace, and the kiss, wow, I head for Wal-Mart, get the film processed, and have the photos in less than two hours.

At six o'clock I call my client, tell her I have the evidence she ask for and she owes me two overnight stays and photography costs, and we setup a meet for nine tonight.

I get home about 11 that night and tell Linda the story; I'm pounding on my chest like a little rooster, strutting around in a barn yard. I really don't know if I ever had surveillance with photo's play out like that before in the last 30 years.

Then there always seems to be a down side to this profession. Something is always happening that seems to take the glitter off what you do. I'm waiting for the other shoe to drop and it always does.

The next day, while at the office I get a phone call from the Sheriff's office in Effingham about the case.

It seems my client took the information I gave her, drove out to the park and to the picnic table where the photographs were taken, waited for the couple to arrive, walked over to them, and shot her husband and his lover to death.

The Sheriff would like to meet with me and take a statement about my surveillance

This is the third time a case has ended this way, I wander if the feeling I had when I took this case was in itself was saying something to me.

Something an Investigator Develops I've been working on developing a sixth sense and this wondering why my client was so cold about this case was a part of my sixth sense development.

It seems from my study the sixth sense begins developing when a person is in their late fifty's or early sixty's. I am getting to the right age!

I believe there is a connection between the sixth sense and some kind of a spiritual connection that develops in a person.

Many investigators call this a hunch, but it is more than that, it is pretty deep feeling that many never acquire, but most women have it by the time they are in their 30's. I found when I go on cases, a woman's sixth sense is usually always right.

When a 30 year old woman says to me "I know this is what is happening." You can almost count on it.

Check, yourself out for the sixth sense, every meet a

person for the first time and have a bad feeling about them?

Ask yourself why and you will find out you were right.

Well this is the way some cases go then there is another, again if everything goes well all will end well. So let's look at this second case.

This was the beginning of a four-year working relationship with the CEO. Assignments throughout the country varied from industrial espionage, to finding lost kids for VIP's.

"I've got something I want you to do, and I need you to start on it to-day."

The Surveillance of Colorado John

Well, I didn't expect this to happen. All the information gathered about this company indicated they always moved slow and had trouble making "now" decisions.

I was used to making "now" decisions and I had a pat answer ready.

"What do you want me to do and when do you want me to start?" I answered without hesitation.

"We have a plant in Nebraska that has large inventory losses. I want you to go up there tomorrow and find out what's going on."

"I'll need access to your plant records and a week to go over the possibly of what maybe happening. I never travel alone, so there will be two of us."

I took my side kick Joe with me; we drove up to the plant in Nebraska and checked into the local Holiday Inn motel. Joe rented a local rent a wreck car, so we would blend in with the local community.

I had just taken delivery on a new Bill Bass series Lincoln Continental, it had a white, fake convertible top and a navy blue bottom, we would have stuck out like we had a sign printed on us, here I am. I went into the plant to meet with the manager, who wasn't to happy to see me, when I presented a letter from the

CEO. "I'll have to call headquarters, and verify this, as he turned and walked away."

Well, at this point the plant manager did not want anyone outside his organization looking into anything. Then I came up with a plan he couldn't refuse.

"Rod, do you have a reward system within your corporation for persons who turn in information resulting in your reduction of losses?"

Rod thought a minute and then stated, "No, we really don't have; but we do have a reward system, up to $50,000; if an employee reports a theft and we find that report is accurate, we pay them 10% of what we estimate the loss would have been."

"Rod, I would like you to make an inquiry with the person who is responsible for that reward fund, and find out if it could be used for a contingency fee to be paid to a private investigator in the event he was able to develop information leading to the arrest of an individual involved in a theft of your product from one of your plants."

Rod said he would check into it and call me back. The following day Rod called and stated that their corporation would be glad to sign a contract with me on the terms used for their employees of 10% of the estimated losses to be paid for information that would develop into the arrest and conviction of parties involved.

I told Rod I would have to think about this for a day and give him a call back. The arrest didn't bother me, it was the conviction that I didn't like. The lawyers could make some kind of a plea deal and cheat me out of my fee.

On the following day I called the plant manager and made arrangements for payment on a performance agreement. I needed some inside help and I put one of my experienced investigators inside the manufacturing plant and they paid him the going rate for those working at the plant.

For three months intelligence information about the operation of this plant was developed. Out of the development of this information, there was only one significant fact we felt we could work with.

Two young employees, working at the lowest pay grade of the corporation in the loading area of rail cars and semi-trucks, seemed to have a considerable amount of money available to them.

I am going to cut the story short, but to give you an idea of what it takes to get a case, run the case and how to get your money is what this is all about.

We all felt that this was the truck we were looking for and this was the employee we had targeted. We decided that we would take the truck to its point of unloading and photograph the unloading operation.

When Colorado John pulled out of that truck stop, we were behind him, confident that we would stay with him wherever he went. From the looks of the tractor trailer unit, we didn't believe the truck could make it to Colorado.

It was an old Peterbilt, at least 25 years old. The fenders flapped as the truck rolled down the highway and the lights bobbed around on the highway as if they were being operated by someone in the cab.

The truck was a dirty green with spots of primer. And when the truck driver was taking on fuel, one of the investigators had an opportunity to look inside the truck. The seats were torn open and the foam rubber was squeezing out of the seams in the seat.

The tires really didn't look that good to us when we first looked at them, but we were later told they were a special radial tire, made particularly for highway driving, with a minimum amount of tread to reduce road friction.

At this point we left the truck stop and the truck seemed to have trouble getting up speed. But once the truck got up speed Colorado John maintained 80 to 85 mph.

About 100 miles out, Colorado John took to some blacktops that were not even on our road atlas. It became necessary for us to shut off the lights on our car in order to follow Colorado John, because there were only two vehicles out there on the road in Nebraska; Colorado John and us.

For five hours that night, we drove with me hanging out of the window on the right hand side of the road looking at the edge of the road, and the driver in solid darkness following my instructions, "go left, left more, hurry up and go left".

After about six hours, Colorado John made a stop in a small town underneath a street light. That gave us a break as John was waiting for daylight.

At the crack of dawn Colorado John started his rig up and began to roll. Even on the blacktops he was running 60 to 70 mph. We followed John for five or six more hours and we realized that John was not going to stop for any more rests and should have plenty of fuel to go where he was going.

In the meantime we began developing a problem— fatigue. We had been on the road working the investigation during the day and that evening when we began the surveillance, we had already had 18 hours in the field.

Now we were running close to 30 hours without sleep, and very little food. We made the decision it would be best if we had Colorado John stopped by the State Police.

We had already determined that we were going to tell the Nebraska State Police that the load on Colorado John's truck was stolen, taking a chance that at least a portion of it was.

As we entered a lazy little town near the border of Nebraska and Colorado, I got on channel 9 of our CB radio and asked for a REACT CB unit to respond.

"Breaker, breaker for REACT unit on channel 9, we have an emergency."

In a few minutes I heard the CB begin to crackle, but I couldn't figure out who was replying to our request for assistance. As we rolled along on that Nebraska blacktop I repeatedly called for assistance on channel 9.

Suddenly I heard, "Go ahead breaker, for REACT on channel 9. This is the Nebraska State Police." I could hardly believe that I had actually picked up the Nebraska State Police headquarters on the REACT, but I advised them that we were representing a corporation in Nebraska and we were following a truck with a stolen load. I couldn't really tell them where I was, but I began giving them landmarks that I would see as we were driving along.

As I looked up ahead I saw a railroad crossing and a huge water tank. I told the State Police dispatcher about the railroad crossing and water tank and immediately he identified our location. Within 15 minutes, in a lonely area of Nebraska, a Nebraska State Police car appeared and stopped the semi.

I had previously worked with Chief of Investigations for the Nebraska State Police in an inquiry concerning the theft. I told the trooper who I had been working with on the Investigation.

He called the Nebraska State Capital and the chief acknowledged that he knew of me and knew I was working on the case. Eager to grab some of the glory, he advised the trooper that he would fly an investigation team to take control of the truck, and that's exactly what happened.

The trooper asked the driver to drive the truck to State Police headquarters. The truck driver refused to do so, locked the cab door and left the truck sitting on the side of the road. The trooper called a wrecker service to tow the truck to their headquarters. The wrecker operator was able to get the truck in neutral, but the truck was so heavy they were unable to move the truck.

The troopers spoke to the truck driver and the truck driver stated he would not drive the truck to the scales. He would give the keys to the State Police and permission to drive the truck if they so desired.

The truck was driven to the State Police scales and it was found that the total weight of the truck and two trailers exceeded 100 tons. This was a load equal to a freight car on the railroad.

I contacted the corporation I was working for and asked

them to obtain a copy of the weight slip. The weight slip showed that the purchase was made for 10 tons of grain, about one tenth of the total truck.

The processed grain that this truck was hauling had a value of $240 per ton. The truck would normally weigh empty about 25 tons, leaving about 75 tons of pay load, far exceeding the legal weight limits for a truck in the state of Nebraska. But even more so, this allowed a theft of 75 tons of processed grain. There was a loss on this one truckload of about, $20,000.00.

(The loading crew would later admit to 20 truckloads they were paid for or about $400, 000, 00 in losses.)

Ok, after three months we had what we needed, now getting paid was the last part of the job.

How I got paid

I made a deal with the CEO, in Decatur, I would make a billing for our normal Investigation rates, that we originally had agreed on, hand carry it to his office, he would make a payment, that day, for the lesser of the two amounts, the regular billing or the 10% of the total loss for the past year ($400,000,00).

My $40,000.00 billing was paid the day presented, and for the remaining cases worked, I was paid the same way, the day he got the billing.

This was an example of two different kinds of surveillances and two different out comes. The big thing about surveillaces, yu never know how the wsill play out or how they will end.

Promise 2, Chapter Two

Skills that might help you on Surveillances

The Mission; each chapter will start with a mission of what we want to accomplish, in the chapter.

In this chapter, we will be talking about Skills that might help someone running surveillance.

A Scenario; a scenario is a story; a story or reference about the subject that you can relate to.

We will use the two stories presented in the last chapter as examples of the surveillances we will be talking about in this chapter.

Details; this will be about the subject and some things you can do.

This surveillance starts with only the details about who is suspected of doing something and you need information before you can start. More important, what skills do you have that will assist you on these surveillances.

This writing plan, will give you an understanding, of what we will be covering in each chapter; it also keeps The Investigator on track when he is writing.

"I love it when a plan comes to-gather"; do you know what TV Series that quote came from? (The "A Team")

What would you have done differently?

At the end of the chapter you might ask yourself, what you would have done based on your past Experiences and Knowledge.

Now, you are the Investigator, Start with writing down anything you are ask,

"Any Question" about as anything about the Investigation, got a recorder? After writing, dictate any thoughts you have to your little hand held recorder.

Then later listen to it, before you start, Does It Make Sense?

Skills, What Kind of Skills would help me?

We are going to talk about investigators since surveillances are investigation related. Everyone has skills of some kind that can be used on surveillance.

The Mission

Let us taken the wander mate in story one who was meeting a nurse once a week. Go to page 10 and read this story again then put yourself in the investigators place and write down your plan for this case. The key to starting any investigation is the plan of how your going to start it.

The Scenario

What made his wife suspicious?

She checked the car mileage, which is simple logic or common sense. She did not get so emotional involved that she could not think.

The same goes for someone running the surveillance. They cannot get emotionally involved in what is going on. So the first skill needed is being able to keep focused on what you are doing.

Suppose the investigator in this case did not state focused on getting the photographs but just had to know what the couple he was surveilling were talking about or what kind of wine they were drinking or what type of food they were snacking on.

Details

Rule & Skill #1 STAY FOCUSED,

Write down why you are doing your surveillance, know why you are doing it and what you want to accomplish. This is a skill and if you do not have it, your surveillance will fail.

This brings us to the next skill needed in surveillance, Logic and Common Sense!

Rule & Skill #2 Logic & Common Sense

Let us take surveillance story #1, the husband loses you when he leaves in the morning, what are you going to do?

1. Stop and think.

2. Take out your written notes and see where he is supposed to be going.

3. Go where he is supposed to be and check, is he there?

4. In this case yes, so now you setup where you can see his car and wait.

This is why you write everything down, keep it with you, and keep focused on what is going on. This is your skill!

Here is a few more Common Sense Skills you should have. If you do not have them begin developing them now.

Can you sit in your car, a coffee shop, cafe, park bench without calling attention to yourself for long periods of time?

Find out by tying it sometime, there is nothing better than having done something before and knowing what it takes.

This is called firsthand knowledge, after you have done it a couple times and you know what you must do it turns into wisdom. You are a wise person who knows what they are doing.

These are a few of the skills needed on a surveillance like the 1st story, the wandering husbnd, every surveillance is different and the person undertaking the task needs to know what skills are needed to do the surveillance before they start one.

What would you have done differently?

Now, after going over your skills and the skill that may help you, What would you have done on this case that would be different? Write it down, look at it, and think about it.

Alright, The Surveillance has started, now what do you need as equipment to get the job done?

"Can you look without the voice in your head commenting, drawing conclusions, comparing, or trying to figure something out?"

— Eckhart Tolle, A New Earth: Awakening to Your Life's Purpose

"This is my secret," he said. "I don't mind what happens."

Promise 3 Chapter Three

Basic Tools You Will Need

The Mission; *each chapter will start with a mission of what we want to accomplish, in the chapter.*

In this chapter we will be talking about people who conduct surveillances and why.

Then some things about surveillances a person should know about before they start surveillance.

Then what kind of equipment will be needed to get the job done.

A Scenario; *a scenario is a story; a story or reference about the subject that you can relate to.*

The surveillance investigation you are thinking about today involves a suspected wayward husband who may be spending time with an unknown person. The story starts on page 10. Read the story and list the equipment you will need.

Details; *this will be about the subject and some things you can do.*

This surveillance starts with only the details about who is suspected of doing something and you need information before you can start.

This writing plan, *will give you an understanding, of what we will be covering in each chapter; it also keeps The Investigator on track when he is writing.*

"I love it when a plan comes to-gather"; do you know what TV Series that quote came from? (The "A Team")

What would you have done differently?

At the end of the chapter you might ask yourself, what

would you have done based on your past Experiences and Knowledge?

Now, you are the Investigator, Start with writing down anything you are ask, "Any Question" about as anything about the Investigation, got a recorder after writing, dictate any thoughts you have to your little hand held recorder. Then later listen to it, before you start, Does It Make Sense?

The Mission

What we want to determine by running this surveillance.

1. Where is the husband going on Tuesday and Thursdays that he puts extra miles on his car?

2. The client wants photographs of anything that is happening.

That is it where is he going and photographers!

The Scenario

The story is on page ten if you need it or by now, they should be in your notebook you have started just for this case.

You are going to start the surveillance Tuesday morning about six a.m., what equipment will you need.

Details

1. We know we need to have a vehicle of some kind.

2. A second person would be nice to have as an observer a cover person if you had to get out and walk.

3. You will need some personal supplies. Some food of some kind. Water to drink, hand wipes for cleanup, somewhere or something to use for personal relief of body fluids.

4. Camera equipment, film, for photographs.

This takes care of basics, but does not for get to have the vehicle ready. A full tank of gas, windows washed so you can take photos out of them, anything else?

All right you have taken care of your personal needs and vehicle, but what about the camera?

What the Investigator is about to recommend is what he has found the best combination of camera, lens, and film for most surveillances involving photographs.

Camera, An auto wind, signal frame, still camera with a format of 35mm for easy film process.

Lens, all lenses must be, as high quality as possible, one 28-80mm, and one 80-200mm lens usually will handle most photograph needs.

Film, The Investigator has found film is his choice for surveillance since it can be controlled by processing it himself if need be.

Well this takes care of basic needs, but there are a lot of things the experienced investigator might include.

A combination of different jackets, coats, and hats in the event he needed to do a walking surveillance.

Just as the scenario story on page 10 played out the investigator needed to change cars and the second story, he had to rent a wreck to blend in with other vehicles.

Well after going over this chapter,

What would you do differently?

At the end of the chapter you might ask yourself, what would you have done based on your past Experiences and Knowledge?

"This is my secret," he said. "I don't mind what happens."

— Eckhart Tolle, A New Earth: Awakening to Your Life's Purpose

"Whenever you become anxious or stressed, outer purpose has taken over, and you lost sight of your inner purpose. You have forgotten that your state of consciousness is primary, all else secondary."

Promise 4, Chapter Four

Who might want Surveillances & Why.

The Mission; each chapter will start with a mission of what we want to accomplish, in the chapter.

In this chapter we will be talking about people who might want a surveillance and why.

Then some things about surveillances a person should know about before they start a surveillance why they want a surveillance is important.

A Scenario; a scenario is a story; a story or reference about the subject that you can relate to.

There will be a couple of short stories about different kinds of surveillance people might want.

Details; this will be about the subject and some things you can do.

Getting the details about a surveillance starts with only the details about who is suspected of doing something.

This writing plan, will give you an understanding, of what we will be covering in each chapter; it also keeps The Investigator on track when he is writing.

"I love it when a plan comes to-gather"; do you know what TV Series that quote came from? (The "A Team")

What would you have done differently?

At the end of the chapter you might ask yourself, what would you have done based on your past Experiences and Knowledge?

Now, you are the Investigator, Start with writing down anything you are ask, "Any Question" about anything about the Investigation, got a recorder, after writing, dictate any thoughts you have to your little hand held recorder. Then later listen to it, before you start, Does It Make Sense?

Who might want Surveillances & Why?

The Mission

In this chapter we will be talking about people who might want a surveillance and why.

Then some things about surveillances a person should know about before they start a surveillance, why they want surveillance is important.

Scenario

We are going to have more than one scenario in this chapter because we are looking at different reasons people want surveillances.

1. Let's start with the most common reason women or men would want their partner followed. Our first story on page 10 tells it "The entire wandering husband,"

2. The story about following the truck on page 17 is one reason businesses wants surveillances. Theft of products of any kind is a reason for watching something or someone.

I had one business client who was losing food in a restaurant. A surveillance was setup after hours and found a cleaning person was removing large amounts of food.

Then there was a case where a large lumber yard was missing many very expense things. We started watch everyone in the business and over a period of weeks it was found people in receiving, storage, at the front gate were all involved in removing ne stoves, refrigerators, television sets and other costly items from the lumberyard.

One day we received a call from a city a 1000 miles away asking for a surveillance of a man's girlfriend, only to find it was a part of a "skimming scam" of gambling proceeds in Vegas.

Finally, a large corporation had us setup a month long watch to determine how many semi-trucks were filled with cases of product. It ended up our client wanted to know if the business was profitable enough for them to start doing the same thing.

We have conducted surveillances by automobile, trucks, on airplanes, at airports, on trains, in hotels hundreds of miles from where we started.

Watching people and things goes on 24/7 you could be watched right now and not know it. Today there are video, electronic surveillances that watch the watchers. Image you take a case of watching someone, only to be watched while you are conducting the surveillance.

If that happens you maybe, setup as a fall guy for something. I have been arrested and put in jail because the client set me up as a diversion and they were stealing a child, kidnapping a person, taking items while the police were busy with arresting me.

As an Investigator I hope that this chapter on "Who would want a surveillance will enlighten you about surveillances and what they may involve.

Details

Each of the examples given should point to a reason you should want details about what you are doing, sign agreements with clients with details of what they want and why.

Now the Investigator is going to tell you why! One of the investigators cases called for a long term surveillance involving a long term client the investigator had done cases for over a period of years.

The client a business person had a "Wandering wife," and millions would be involved in any settlement in the event of a divorce. The surveillance became involved when it was found the wife was involved with a state drug enforcement officer.

As the months moved on the case involved air travel, long ground surveillances, unknown electronic and video surveillances. Then an involvement of the wife and officer selling drugs, it dragged people in behind all of this and the Investigator had documentation of what was going on.

When this was found out the Investigator, conducting the surveillance was attacked by the legal system, which was costly and ended in a great loss to the investigator conducting the surveillance.

Details a needed, but sometimes a client may say, "No thanks I don't want to do that," great let them go elsewhere!

What would you have done differently?

At the end of the chapter you might ask yourself, what would you have done based on your past Experiences and Knowledge?

Promise 5, Chapter Five

Ideas on How to start the Surveillance

The Mission; each chapter will start with a mission of what we want to accomplish, in the chapter.

In this chapter we will be talking about how you might start your surveillance investigation.

A Scenario; a scenario is a story; a story or reference about the subject that you can relate to.

The surveillance investigation your thinking about today involves a suspected wayward husband who may be spending time with an unknown person.

These principles will apply to starting any surveillance investigation.

Details; this will be about the subject and some things you can do.

This surveillance starts with only the details about who is suspected of doing something and you need information before you can start.

This writing plan, will give you an understanding, of what we will be covering in each chapter; it also keeps The Investigator on track when he is writing.

"I love it when a plan comes to-gather"; do you know what TV Series that quote came from? (The "A Team")

What would you have done differently?

At the end of the chapter you might ask yourself, what would you have done based on your past Experiences and Knowledge?

Now, you are the Investigator, Start with writing

down anything you are ask, "Any Question" about as anything about the Investigation, got a recorder after writing, dictate any thoughts you have to your little hand held recorder. Then later listen to it, before you start, Does It Make Sense?

The Mission

How you might start surveillance

The Investigator will discuss a couple of ways you could start a surveillance investigation.

A Scenario; a scenario is a story; a story or reference about the subject that you can relate to.

The surveillance investigation you are thinking about today involves a suspected wayward husband who may be spending time with an unknown person. Story on page 10.

These principles will apply to starting any surveillance investigation.

Details; this will be about the subject and some things you can do.

This surveillance starts with only the details about who is suspected of doing something and you need information before you can start.

What would you have done differently?

At the end of the chapter you might ask yourself, what would you have done based on your past Experiences and Knowledge?

Starting a surveillance Investigation

Let us start with our *scenario story* on page 10..

Details, we have a wife, she has information indicating her husband puts more miles on his car on Tuesday and Thursday.

She suspects he is spending time with a nurse, he leaves home at 6 a.m. to go to the hospital.

The wife wants photographs of what is going on after he leaves home.

To start with, you need information about everything. This is where you start your notebook on this case. The notebook can be one of those little pocket note books for the dollar store. Who cares, it is your notes that go into your file when this surveillance is over, the notebook is your protection in case your client comes back with you did not do what I ask.

1. Why do you want surveillance?

Well we know what the wife wants, now we have to get down to the business of running a moving vehicle surveillance to a place and from there it could be anything. A walk, a game of golf, a walk to a local pub or in the park, we just do not know what will happen.

2. What is goals on time, expenses, and distances.

We have set limits with the wife, follow the husband two days. We have settled on money and have a check for the next two days work.

3. Who or what are you watching.

We know the car we will be following and we have to "Assume" whoever is driving this car is the Husband.

4. What does the surveillance require in manpower, equipment, and time.

Now we have to start making decisions on what we will be wearing, the car we will be driving and if we will need another person to assist.

With this information, you must take the time to assemble what you will need to run the surveillance.

At this point what would you do on this surveillance knowing your now skills.

Write it down

This would be the only way the Investigator would recommend starting a surveillance. The only other way would be meeting a drunk in a tavern, taking a few bucks to do something and hope that something, whatever you did will be ok.

Promise 6, Chapter Six

Tips on walking, moving & vehicle Surveillance.

The Mission; *each chapter will start with a mission of what we want to accomplish, in the chapter.*

In this chapter we will be talking about different kinds of surveillance and some things you can do while on the surveillances.

Then some things about surveillances a person should know about before they start a surveillance.

A Scenario; *a scenario is a story; a story or reference about the subject that you can relate to.*

The surveillance investigation your thinking about today involves different scenarios for different surveillances.

Details; *this will be about the subject and some things you can do.*

This surveillance starts with scenarios with only the details about who is and what they suspected of.

This writing plan, *will give you an understanding, of what we will be covering in each chapter; it also keeps The Investigator on track when he is writing.*

"I love it when a plan comes to-gather"; do you know what TV Series that quote came from? (The "A Team")

What would you have done differently?

At the end of the chapter you might ask yourself, what would you have done based on your past Experiences and Knowledge?

Now, you are the Investigator, Start with writing

down anything you are ask, "Any Question" about as anything about the Investigation, got a recorder after writing, dictate any thoughts you have to your little hand held recorder. Then later listen to it, before you start, Does It Make Sense?

This section is for an Investigator who may not have a lot of knowledge about the subject of Surveillance, Observation, and Activity Checks. We will describe the different uses and how the Investigators can use them.

SURVEILLANCES, OBSERVATIONS AND ACTIVITY CHECKS

There is a lot to be said for the use of surveillance, observation and activity checks in determine what an individual is doing.

In most instances, without going to the field and actually observing a person, it is difficult to determine what they are doing.

A professional investigator has the skills and experience to conduct surveillances and observations, but there are times when this specialized area of investigation cannot be used.

Keep in mind at all times, that investigators are not miracle makers, and the difficulty factor of most surveillances is high.

The investigator will need as much information as possible concerning the person who will be the target of the investigation. Full name, middle initial, proper spelling of last name, addresses, date of birth, physical description, Social Security number, family status, family background information, vehicles driven and available to the person, and personal habits will all help the investigator in the field achieve the results desired.

Every successful surveillance, observation, or activity check requires some initial research and layout on the part of the investigator. In most instances it takes as much time and effort to lay out a small one day observation, as it does one that might last two or three weeks.

As a professional investigator, I require that every surveillance, observation, or activity check be laid out by an investigator who has at least ten years' experience in the field and has worked hundreds of such cases.

This person will have the ability to size up the area where the investigation will take place and determine the type of equipment and quality of investigator that will be required.

The agent in charge of this operation will lay out the entire surveillance and brief the field investigator before the surveillance, observation or activity check begins.

The investigator in the field must have the right equipment for the job. This requires that investigators maintain a fleet of surveillance vehicles that blend into all areas and provide the proper cover for an undetected surveillance.

This equipment begins with the vehicle the investigator will be using. It must be fully equipped for communication, a prolonged period of observation, and sufficient power supplies for the use of specialized equipment.

The reason that equipment is so important is the acceptability of the area where the surveillance, observation, or activity check may be. In one area, a van may be of use. In another, an older car sitting in a parking lot may be just the thing; or in a rural area, a pickup truck.

The equipment cannot be too old or too new. It must blend in and be a part of its surroundings. Photography is used in all instances during the investigation. This is not just for the client, but also for the investigator to use in the office and photos become a part of the file, providing proof the investigator was there.

The investigators may not always be able to photograph the target of the investigation in some activity, but basic recognition of vehicles, housing and areas where the target frequents, are used for record of the investigation and future investigation periods.

There is times that no matter what investigators do, they do not blend in to their surroundings and cannot be fruitful in their search for information.

Generally, the agent in charge of the layout can recognize these problems and suggest alternates to the investigator in the field. There are times when there are no alternates and when these occasions arise, the client, will be contacted and informed of this difficulty factor.

In most instances, some information on the habits and movements of an individual will be obtained. Whether or not photographs and details will be obtained depends on the circumstances involved in the surveillance.

I always like to inform my clients that surveillances, observations and activity checks are the most time consuming, expensive, and non-productive methods of obtaining information in the investigation field. However, usually by the time the client comes to us, they have exhausted every other means of obtaining information.

We understand this, but please understand our position. If you have exhausted every means of obtaining information, remember the difficulty factor of the surveillance, observation, and activity check is high, even when we are successful.

The Report

The report not only gives you a record of what has been found during the investigation, but lets you know what the investigators have done and provides you with a permanent record for the future, in the event you might want to forward this investigation to another agency or place it in the hands of an in—house investigator for follow up.

Now let us talk about some of the things you might be doing on surveillance.

Individuals and corporations to develop information on a need to know basis use surveillances, observations, and activity checks, in many ways. In most cases, this type of investigation service is used as a last resort; or on a single occasion when nothing else will seem to work.

Moving surveillances of individuals are conducted to see whom they contact and what they do. This type of surveillance is used for delivery trucks that have had high losses or employees entrusted with equipment who might be misusing it.

There are many reasons to use surveillance to obtain information. Observations and activity checks are used primarily to obtain information on what is happening at a given location.

It might be an individual's home who is on compensation due to a personal injury at work, yet they are painting their house, digging holes for foundations, building garages, as well as repairing cars and chopping firewood for their neighbors.

Whatever it might be, observations and activity checks often are fruitful in developing information. Investigators always like to tell a few "weird stories."

Since 1951, I have conducted and laid out thousands of surveillances, observations, and activity checks. Here a few stories that might be of interest to you.

In 1951, I was working for the Division of Forestry, State of Illinois, as a forest fire fighter. It was an extremely bad year for forest fires and suddenly there appeared to be a rash of forest fires in a given area.

I knew nothing of surveillance, yet the staff foresters instructed me to find out what happened. This is where my first surveillance began. I went to the most likely area where a fire might start. I dug a "foxhole," camouflaged myself, and sat in the hole.

Three days later a car drove up, a person got out of the car and began setting a fire. I obtained a description of the individual, automobile, and license number. After the fire was extinguished, I returned to headquarters with the information.

It seems that due to the intense fire danger, reporters from throughout the Midwest had converged on the area to photograph the fires and write news headlines concerning the loss in Illinois each day.

It was found from the information obtained through my stakeout, that the individual who set the fire was a reporter in need of some quick photographs, and some news input to his newspaper.

On one occasion, I spent a year on surveillance for a major corporation. They estimated that for a number of years they had lost $100,000 a day in products. They had, had investigators in the past but they had not been successful in locating the loss. The opportunity was offered to me and I accepted it.

Making a long story short, I started with an investigation of research and layout, which the corporation did not agree with. They felt investigators should get in their car and drive around.

I spent about two weeks in their office with their records and began my field investigation. Everywhere I turned, things just did not seem to be right. The records indicated one thing, but the physical indicated another.

This investigation called for a surveillance of a manufacturing plant, the transportation of products by railroad cars to river barges where the material was loaded on barges and went to New Orleans.

The barges sat in storage for a period of time and then were taken to ships where the product was loaded onto the ships and taken to a foreign country. The loss seemed to occur when the weights were taken at the final destination by the purchaser.

The reason this investigation took a year was simply the variables that were involved. But after a methodic check of each stage of manufacture and transportation, a solution was found.

Product was being lost everywhere; in the manufacturing stages, it was a scale that was weighing the product wrong, in the transportation by railroad cars in ill repair, in the poorly supervised loading operation at the river, and by theft in the rail yard and barge storage. Overall, we were able with the help of photographs and video tapes, to see where the loss occurred.

It took this company more than a year to close the doors to this loss and the results were due to surveillance and observation.

I could go on and tell you about an arsonist who was a police officer, of another arsonist who was the manager of a security company who set fires to buildings and property and was made a hero by putting the fires out.

I could tell you about the many cargo thefts that were detected by long term and long range surveillance of semi trucks where photographic evidence was obtained of theft in the loading process, theft in the transportation between points, and theft at the receiving point.

And then there are the hundreds of compensation cases, where on a single drive by, photographs were taken of individuals who claimed total disability, who were 20 feet in the air painting their home, or operating snow removal equipment for hours on end.

There are thousands of uses for surveillance by individuals and corporations. I really do not have a "hit" rate as such concerning surveillances, since each surveillance is an individual occurrence with a completely different set of factors.

But I really must tell you one more story about a major paving contractor who suddenly could not seem to properly estimate the cost on major highway projects. When the CEO of this company came to me and explained his problem, it took us a week to analyze, and realize what was happening.

There were so many precautions taken against someone else finding out what the bid was, that the CEO felt there was not any way a person could obtain information.

Finally a suspected employee was baited, a surveillance set up, and it was found that the night before a bid was to be made, this individual always made a phone call to, and met with a person from, a competitive company. It was at this point we were able to rush in and obtain evidence that the individual was passing on bid information to the competition.

And then there is the individual who violated his

noncompetitive agreement and opened his own company; and there was the man who hid his assets from his partners; and also the one where both partners were stealing equipment from each other.

So in summary, surveillance pays, but only if it is properly conducted with quality investigators and equipment.

Investigators are used for a variety of reasons. Some for background checks, information gathering, research, technical accident investigation and reconstruction, criminal defense and crime scene searches; but then there is a side of investigation that few persons think of using an investigator for. It is that inner feeling that tells you that something is wrong; that search for inner peace of mind.

Investigators have mixed feelings concerning requests for investigations; that inner self, who senses something, is not exactly what it is. Many inquiries are for peace mind, a feeling of something is wrong. On the top of the list of peace investigations are marital partners, wanting to know what their partner is doing.

Second on are insurance companies who have received a call from neighbors or friends of an individual who has been injured and they report to the insurance company the individual is faking the injury.

Last on the list, are businesses suspecting employee theft, checks of unsupervised employees, missing property within the company, takeovers that are rumored, and a variety of incidentals that affect the leadership of a business organization?

This section is written to cover all three areas from which we receive investigation requests, since all of them have a common denominator; that being a person who is the figure of the inquiry, one who is human and makes mistakes.

Promise 7, Chapter Seven

Some ideas on Photographing & Surveillance.

STILL OR MOVING PHOTOGRAPHY:

Both still and moving photography should be done by a knowledgeable individual who can present himself in the courtroom in a manner of professionalism. A record should be kept of all photographs and moving pictures taken, recording the date, time, and what the subject was.

The surveillance photographer should have quality equipment and be experienced in surveillance photography to obtain the needed evidence.

Surveillance photography is a specialized field and the majority of persons who are experienced in the use of a camera are not experienced enough to perform surveillance photography. Surveillance photography is performed under the most trying conditions.

I began working surveillances in the year 1959. In that period of time the 4 x 5, graphic camera was the stock and trade of the crime-scene technician and the professional photographer in the police field.

Few attachments were available for the camera and the size of the camera prevented its use except in a specialized van or house area where it could be readily concealed.

During the last 50 years, camera developments in the 35 mm field have continued and the standard for a professional photographer in the investigation field today is the 35 mm camera.

35 mm camera accessories are readily available through catalog or local photography outlets.

Telephoto lens in the 100 and 200 mm areas are readily available and affordable to the private investigator. There are special techniques needed for using surveillance lenses, but these techniques can be readily acquired by most investigators.

I can recall using the 16 mm Bollix camera for moving pictures in investigations 50 years ago. The 16 mm camera was as large as a professional video camera and required constant winding to keep the film moving.

A three lens turret provided zoom-in capability, but the photographer was required to have the skills of a motion picture studio technician to come home with pictures of a quality that could be identified. Today, video tape provides the field investigator with a compact, low-level light.

So let us talk about what you know about cameras and Photography. There are all kinds of photography training material available, but most of all you have to know your camera like it is a personal friend.

You talk to it, you know ever like thing about it, what it will and will not do. Really you need a group of friend cameras to get the photography assignment do right.

You are going to need still and moving pictures. You will need different cameras for different jobs, different lens, and other accessories that will allow you to get the job done.

A small pocket camera that is with you all the time. The work horse that can take being dropped, riding in the truck of your car, one that can take heat, and freezing weather.

A camera friend that can be charged in the car, run long periods without care, one that fits into your hand like putting on a comfortable glove.

Scenario's about Photography

The conditions photography is taken under will determine the quality of the photo.

Your photo is taken through glass and the glass is dirty, has raindrops on it, the glass is tinted, or of poor quality, that will make the difference in how the photography comes out.

Let us say you are on a bus, train, or plane and it is

sharking as it moves along what will it do to your photography?

Better yet you're in a bad lighting condition, one minute there is bright sun light, reflective sand or windshields of automobiles, and there are shadows, dim lighting, what can you do?

Well in most instances nothing, but then again if you know your camera, film, and filers a lot can be done.

What happens if you are in a people place and you have to use a tiny camera, use cover of people and other things to get that one shot you have been waiting on.

Remember the story on page 10 about the once in a lifetime photographic assignment, everything was perfect, it never happened before or after that.

So from experience I can tell you will be taking photos, while your standing, sitting, lying down, and on the move.

You will be in hospitals, movie theaters, taverns, and little cafes taking pictures through windows, in the rain, on the beach, and places you wonder why you are there, that is all of what surveillance photography is!

"You become most powerful in whatever you do if the action is performed for its own sake rather than as a means to protect, enhance, or conform to your role identity."

— *Eckhart Tolle, A New Earth: Awakening to Your Life's Purpose*

"Authentic human interactions become impossible when you lose yourself in a role."

Summary

Well, we have had our coffee and talked about how one could go into the private detective business or become an investigator in some specialized field.

I hope we have covered most of the information you are interested in and you have a good idea of what it would take to start conducting surveillance.

Investigation surveillances like most any profession takes some kind of skill. Basic skills can be acquired by reading, watching videos, and in classroom at learning centers, but to my knowledge, there is no one or no training in how you can startup a Private Detective business out of your living room or car on a cell phone or i-pad.

Someone really interested in starting without a big cash layout and having enough reserve cash to live on for say a year, should be able to map out route to becoming or at least realizing they do not want to become a Private Detective.

I am going to finish with one last story on How To Acquire an Investigation Specialty.

At the end of each of this series, I tell this story to encourage those who want to be the best they can to seek out specialized training in their field.

There is someone, somewhere, hidden back in the corner of some business complex that offers specialized training just like Dektor, and then they are not there anymore.

Secret Agents, Spies, and other Stuff
A place called Dektor

I had a few thousand in the bank and that would allow me to go to Dektor in Maryland to pickup some new equipment and get some training.

Dektor was a place where spies for all over the world trained and when you purchased equipment, it came with training and some contracts to help you pay for it.

I was told originally President Kennedy formed Dektor during the Cuban crisis in the period we were near a Third World War over Russia being in Cuba, which was only 90 miles away, with missile sites.

In the 1960's Dektor was to design special equipment to secure communications for the President and his other communications with the military.

After this was all over Dektor continued to develop equipment, for use by all investigation agencies, private and government all over the world.

It was going to take a couple weeks of training and to get the equipment, since each piece of equipment was hand built while you were training in the use.

I wanted to get in a specialty area of services and already had expertise in using some equipment as an LEIU Agent when in the State Police Detective Section.

After returning from Dektor, it was not long before I was doing audio countermeasures cases around the country. For an investigator to specialize in a given area charges the picture of what they do, who they do it for, and what they charge.

When I was a LEIU Agent with the State Police, I had been trained by the Justice Department in the use of special wiretapping equipment and acted as the "Expert" for the ISP Detective Section.

I thought maybe doing this type of services work be better

for me to enter, since I already had firsthand knowledge of what was involved in the process.

In my search, I found companies who sold the equipment, but most of it was bordering on being junk. One company I came across sounded as if they might have what I needed; training in "How to" and later I found they had a get history in audio countermeasures to back up their claims.

Dektor a name I had never heard before was that company. It was rumored Dektor trained spies from all over the world in Audio countermeasures and made custom equipment and it was expensive.

It was said Dektor required training for all equipment purchased, taking about two weeks to manufacture the equipment and finish the training.

I inquired by phone, but they said I would have to appear in person at their headquarters' in Maryland, just outside of Washington D.C. before they would consider selling their equipment and training me.

My trip to Washington DC

This trip was more like a TV thriller than a movie, the cab driver knows more about where I am going than I do. It reminded me of when I was working on riverboats and I would be roaming around river front areas in places like New Orleans at midnight looking for a warehouse office. You would think I was on some kind of secret mission in another country

The key again is getting a guide if you do not where you are and what is happening around you. A sure bet in a major city is an American cab driver, you speak the same language, they understand you and you understand them. I have found in my travels in major cities most of the cab drivers are someone brought in by the Government as refuge and put in jobs by the government.

It sounded like what I wanted and needed so, I flew into D.C. and caught a cab. I gave the cab driver the address in Maryland; he looked at it and ask me if I was one of those

"Spooks" that was going to the warehouse.

When we arrived in the area, the cab driver drove into what was a manufacturing industrial complex of maybe dozen three-story brick buildings; it looked very much like a military complex.

"OK, Buddy. Which one are you going to?" The cab driver said

As I looked at the building, I did not know what to say.

Looking back over his shoulder the driver ask, "This your first time here?"

Leaning forward, "Yes it is and I really don't know where to go."

"If you have never been here before, all the new people go to the D Building and go into the blue door."

Still leaning forward,

"Do you come here often?"

"Every once in a while, yea."

"What is this place, do you know?"

"I think it is some kind of a secret place for the CIA."

"Why do you think that?"

"Because Guys like you come here all the time."

As the cab was leaving, I was entering the Blue door. The inside of the building was an open space; it looked like it may have been a factory at one time, but now it was empty.

The office area consisted of a large wooden table with a dozen chairs around it. On the table were stacks of what looked like files, not in folders. Seated at the table were two men dressed in white shirts and ties loosened and pulled away from their necks.

I spent the next four hours answering and asking questions, when I was through they said they would get a hold of me and let me know if they would sell me the equipment and prove training to use it.

They gave me a price of $10,000 cash in front, for two weeks, training, and equipment I would need to do the work.

I caught a fight back to Chicago, leaving New York at eleven. When I got back to Springfield, it took me a day to figure out what really went on in D.C. The truth is I really never figured it out until later, what I thought was happening was not really happening at all.

Dektor calls me back a week later

It was a week later when I got a message to call a phone number in Washington D.C., when I answered the call I got a voice message to call another number after twelve midnight the next day. I thought,

"Come on, how many people do business after twelve Midnight?"

When I made the after twelve midnight call I hooked up to a real person who said they were waiting for my call. I was instructed on how to move the $10,000 and they said when it was done they would contact me with instructions.

Sound like a secret agent movie? Well it is like a movie and it is hard for most to believe there is a secret world most do not know about in the private sector.

It was two days after "Moving the Money" and I received a call though my answering service on what to do Who, What, Where, and Why.

To make it short, Dektor would pay for everything, first I was to take a flight out of St Louis, there would be transportation at the Airport on arrival, and they would take care of housing and meals for the next two weeks. The last instruction was to dress casual, just like I would be doing some hands, and knees work.

I arrived at the airport and picked up my tickets, as I went through inspection, I was told to step over to the side and went to a table where I would be processed. A person who identified himself as a federal agent hand searched my bag and had me sign a release.

From this point on everything went smooth, I arrived at the same building complex as before, but went into a Green door, now this was more like a business. It was still an old warehouse, but jazzed up a little, colored walls, some carpeting, good lighting, and everything on location.

One thing that was obvious, there were twenty people staying here and most likely receiving training of some kind, for a piece of equipment they would be taking home with them.

Everything was secret something, so I ask my instructor about what was going on, who was Dektor?

He was able to answer most of my questions freely. He started by,

"Was, and was is a good question. Dektor was a special unit of the CIA and was funded by order of President Kennedy during the Cuban Missile Crisis in the early 1960's to design and manufacture Audio Countermeasures equipment for the CIA and FBI because they wanted to secure communications during the Missile Crisis.

Training Center for the Worlds Spies

After the assassination of President Kennedy the funding continued and Dektor operated until the funding stopped, then the employees purchased the name and kept designing equipment and selling the equipment and training as contractors to the government and select persons around the world."

Well, that was the story about Dektor I was given and I never heard anything else about it. The big secrecy about keeping everything under their control was the people they trained were used while they were training to check government offices for listening devices and they did not want the information when, where and how leaked, because we did find phone taps and room bugs when we were checking.

Classes were held nine to eleven and one to three in the daylight, then ten to two at night it was the real thing, running countermeasures in government offices.

The Night work was the reason for all the secret stuff in the beginning and on coming to training. You had a top security clearance run on you before you came and were never allowed to make a phone call or leave after you arrived.

After attending the training at Dektor I received, a few phone calls from persons who felt they were under attack by someone using audio over hear devices in their homes, cars and businesses.

How they knew about me and the services I offered in Countermeasures field is unknown to me, as I never advertised this service. I always felt Dektor had made a referral to those inquiring about someone to perform a Countermeasures sweep.

For Charlie this opened an entirely new business over the coming year and Charlie would be in over his head most of the time. But, Charlie being from the World War Two period and seeing how nothing was impossible every Saturday afternoon for all his hero's and the British Commando's he always came out alive.

The reason for this story about Detor was to show how things change and your directions change with them. Now I was going to do electronic surveillances inside buildings, there would be a need for more equipment and the way the surveillance would be run. My job now to catch the person that is doing the electronic surveillance by using Countermeasures equipment to detect an electronic surveillance.

I had been on my trip to Dektor in D.C. for two weeks and was not allowed to use a phone. When I got back, there were a lot of fires to put out in Springfield.

I had forgotten about Alex and out trip to Ashland. Alex figured Alex would have trouble collecting his money, but I knew he would pay me when he could.

Alex pays me for the KY Trip

I am at one of my Security locations the Holiday Inn, there having a few problems with the new night manager who unmistakably thinks him in charge of security and feel the officers should have additional duties, like taking meals up to rooms and picking up dirty trays in the hallways.

Its Alex calling me on my bag phone, my God I have not turned the phone on until today it has been two weeks, I will bet Alex has been calling me on this number.

"Alex, where have you been?"

"Where have I been, where have you been?"

"Why haven't you called the office or the answering service number I gave you?"

"I don't have any other number except this one. The guys at the towing company in Cincinnati stole all my stuff out of the car and this is the only number I carried on me."

"Charlie I have the money I owe you and I need to tell you about all the stuff that happen in the last month, how about meeting me South of Bloomington, at the truck stop, and I'll tell you all about it?"

"When do you want to meet?"

"How about in 3 hours, that will be about midnight?"

"Alex, I don't want to do this."

"I am on my way down to western Tennessee, I can go down I-55 to Bloomington, meet you, and then cut over to I-57.

I'll be gone for a couple weeks and I don't want to take a chance of losing your money while I'm down there."

"OK Alex, I'm going to get Joe to go with me and he can drive back, See you at midnight."

It took almost an hour to get Joe and head north on I-55, we got to the truck stop right at midnight. Joe stayed in the car and slept in the back seat, while I went in to talk to Alex.

Now this is truly something out of the old James Cagney movies, two guys who are broke most of the time talking big money in a cheap food place and act like they really believe it.

Alex was smiling as he watched me approach the booth he was in. He had already been to the all you can eat buffet and had three plates spread out on the table.

"Hey Charlie good to see you, I got here early and I hadn't eaten since noon, so I started eating as soon as I got here."

"Alex I don't think I will be eating anything, I'm really tired and I haven't slept much in the last three days I just drove back from D.C., Joe is out in the back seat of the car asleep, he is going to drive back."

"So why are you going down in Tennessee?"

"While I was in Ashland I met some people and their family was in an accident, the car blew up and they were burned really badly.

It's a Ford car and there is a big nationwide suite going on gas tank mounts, Jay said he would give ten thousand if I got them to sign a contract."

"What do you think your chances are to get a contract signed?"

"Pretty good, the people I met gave me a call today and ask me to come down as soon as I could, I told them not to talk to anyone and I would be there in the morning."

"You think Jay is really going to pay you for this one?"

"He gave me five thousand in front, what do you think?"

"Sounds good to me."

"So what went on in Ashland, after I Left?"

"Charlie order something to eat, you look tired and this is going to take a few minutes."

Alex motions to the waitress.

"OK, I'd like to have a full order of biscuits & gravy, and coffee."

Alex reaches into his shirt pocket and pulls out folded

money and hands it to me.

"This is the $3500.00 I owe you on the Ashland trip."

In the money was a big bill.

"A $1000.00 bill, what the hell am I going to do with a bill like that?"

Alex smiles, "You could always give the waitress a good tip."

"Alex cut the crap, if I showed at the bank with a $1000.00 bill they would call the feds in and I'd be answering questions."

"Have somebody else to take it in and get change."

"Take this back and give me something else right now"

"I can't, Jay paid me in $1000.00 bills, if I didn't take it I'd never get it."

"This isn't funny money is it?"

"No, no, that's all he had on him when I went to the office tonight."

"How many of these things have you got on you?"

"This is the only one left, Jay called the Check Cashing and told them to cash them out, but they didn't have enough money."

"Alex this looks and sounds like a setup, I'll take this but if it's bad, you still owe me."

"It's alright; I cashed four of them tonight."

"Yea, at Jay's money store, he might have done it so he could move some money onto the street."

If you have not noticed, Private Detectives only meet new clients in their office. Unlike police if you just want to talk about it you will be meeting in a little restaurant somewhere convenient, it is your only way to have privacy. It is the old saying, even the walls have ears.

"OK, tell me what happened at Ashland?"

"Well remember Joseph? He picked me up Sunday after

you left and stopped by his church on the way to pickup his car.

We went inside and there were not any seats, it was just a big building with wood floors and everyone was staggering around with their hands in the air and singing.

Then they brought out this big wooden box, set it down and took the lid off and it was full of rattlesnakes, and the snakes started crawling out of the box. People stated picking the snakes up and holding them in the air.

I just stood there and these snakes were everywhere, so I wanted to get out of there and I started shuffling my feet and moving toward the door.

Somehow, one of the snakes wrapped around my ankle and they could not get it off and it bit me. I was in the hospital for two days and my leg was swelled up for a week.

Alex getting into his story. That is not all of what happened.

"Come on what else happened."

"Well you know that mountain of coal the group in Chicago bought through the Attorney at Ashland, I went out to find it, and it was already mined, all that was left was a mountain of rock.

The Attorney scammed them, and they sent some guys down to get their money and the attorney skipped out.

They gave me my money anyway, and thanked me."

"How are you feeling now?"

"Good, as good as new."

It was three when I left Alex, Joe drove back to Springfield, parked the car in front of my apartment and left me asleep in the back seat, I woke up when someone tapped on the window, and waved at me.

Charlie and Alex never thought about how what they were doing looked to those around them when they were talking about what they were or planning something.

As Charlie thinks back on the many times they were in little restaurants and their server would be in on what was being said, money changing hands and how they looked in suits hanging out in night places like truck stops? Oh, my God what a mess they are!

I could tell you about a couple of more things that happened right after I met Alex at the Truck stop, but that is not why we met for coffee, maybe next time when we met we both can share what happened on our most recent cases.

Bye for now, your friend Charles Neuf, The Investigator

"Nonresistance, nonjudgment, and nonattachment are the three aspects of true freedom and enlightened living."

— Eckhart Tolle, A New Earth: Awakening to Your Life's Purpose

www.ingramcontent.com/pod-product-compliance
Lightning Source LLC
Chambersburg PA
CBHW051412250726
48655CB00003B/1014